HOW TO HOLD A
BETTER MEETING

by FRANK SNELL

Illustrations by Rupert Witalis

CORNERSTONE LIBRARY • NEW YORK

Reprinted 1968

CORNERSTONE LIBRARY PUBLICATIONS
are distributed by
Simon & Schuster, Inc.
630 Fifth Avenue
New York, New York 10020

Manufactured in the United States of America
under the supervision of
Rolls Offset Printing Co., N. Y.

||| CONTENTS

CONTENTS

IIII PREFACE

This book was not designed primarily as a class-room text, although the need exists there equally. It was written to be carried in the pocket of all businessmen to be read on the 5:35. It was written for the executive who faces four hours of meetings starting at 9:15 tomorrow—a day he desperately needs to use for catching up. This book was written to be applied immediately.

If teachers of classes in meeting and conference techniques decide to use these ideas, we will be doubly grateful. There is no priority on the solving of the meeting problem. It is the most pressing dilemma of today's business. Whoever contributes to its solution deserves our thanks and praise.

These words come not only from the author of this book. They come from the businessman who desperately seeks to avoid the third ragged meeting of the day!

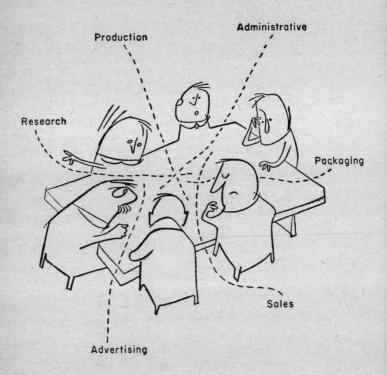

Research

Production

Administrative

Packaging

Sales

Advertising

"I cannot tell you *what* to determine, but if you please I will tell you *how*."

—BENJAMIN FRANKLIN,

in answer to a request for advice from Joseph Priestly in 1772.

IIII GUIDEPOSTS

This book points out directional signs which lead to direct talk in meetings. It will show you how to be a better leader. It will suggest ways of calling a conference and ways of guiding it to a successful conclusion. It will outline the best type and length of your contribution. It will point out different forms of leadership and review the ones best suited to business. It will expose many ways to make your next meeting more fruitful and direct.

It is not a substitute for premeeting preparation!

IIII ON TALKING TOGETHER

The growth of man has been largely determined by his ability to make himself understood. By his built-in desire to talk *about* things. By his desire to pass ideas to others. This will to communicate is what has made man more than the animals.

The growth of today's business is also governed by this ability to communicate—the ability to coördinate, mold, and apply the thinking of its individual members through effective talking together.

There is very little of your working day when you are not concerned with ideas, decisions, and actions which will have a direct effect on the development and future of your company.

And 90 percent of this activity is carried on orally!

Your personal success and the success of your company will be determined largely by the success of people talking together. In particular, by successful face-to-face talking around the meeting table.

|||| THE MEETING — AND
YOUR COMPANY

The meeting? Who needs it! that's easy . . . everybody! Eventually.

The meeting is an indispensable tool working for you and your company every day. You can't work without it. On this everyone is agreed. Unfortunately, it is also the one business activity that receives little or no planned attention. No one seems to know *how* to make it work better.

After all, talking is a natural function. "Like eating. Do it all the time." It's hard to step back and look objectively at an activity so much a part of us. What can you learn about talking?

A great deal! And the first thing is to recognize that people must *learn* to talk together efficiently.

Unlike Topsy, good group talking won't just grow.

The meeting is like the weather: everybody talks about it, about how many meetings are called, about how few meetings come to decisions, etc., but no one attacks the problem directly. That is the sole purpose of this book . . . to help you *do* something about *your* leadership and *your* meetings in *your* company.

‖‖ THE MEETING—WHAT IS IT?

A meeting is several people gathered in the office of Bill Anderson to talk out a problem on distribution. A meeting is a supervisor and three junior executives in a Thursday morning "brainstorming" session. A meeting is a report by production on the new package being designed for your product.

A meeting is a group talking together *with a clearly defined purpose in mind*.

Business and industry are growing so rapidly that they are bringing to light new and difficult problems. Like an army slashing quickly into new territory, today's business is running ahead of its communication. The ways of passing information *must* be improved to maintain the pace.

This is why the meeting has become so important.

11

The executive doesn't have time to write *or* read all the memos that pile up every day. You can't get the thinking of a group on the phone. The meeting alone can handle this business growth and fulfill the need for better communication. Unfortunately, good meetings are not just there for the asking. It takes a clearly defined form and then practice to make them better!

Look at it this way. We work out the problems of distribution down to the last district. We lay out plans which will gain dealer support of our product. We look at shipments, consumer research, product design, competition, etc. Every step in the marketing of a product is carefully analyzed, evaluated, and a plan laid out to reduce the possibility of error. Evaluated to insure success.

What about the meeting situation? What's being done here? Most executives will admit they spend most of their time working together, coördinating thinking, and applying the results. The fact is that the average executive may spend 50 percent of his working day in meetings . . . talking ideas.

Have you personally ever heard of anyone lay-ing out a plan for more direct, pleasant, *efficient* meeting methods? Methods that work?

Business today is too big for one person to have all the answers. This means you'll hear the cry, "Let's call a meeting," more and more often. If you can make that meeting work better, you will be a more valuable member of your organization.

IIII WHAT CAN THE MEETING DO BETTER?

Aldous Huxley, the famous philosopher, has said, "The great end of life is not knowledge, but action." And he is absolutely right. Ideas are made to be applied.

No one would suggest the meeting as a replacement for the individual decision-maker. No one wants to replace him. No one could! There is no doubt that *one* man can make a decision faster than any meeting devised.

However, the meeting can do things he cannot. And, do them far better. That is why the meeting has been called the center pin of business and industry.

The following are reasons why:

—It is the fastest way of passing information to a group of people.

—It is the surest way of being positive that everyone understands equally what

14

has been presented. The best way of holding misunderstandings to a minimum.

—It can literally save you days of time. Time wasted in the sending and answering of endless memos and letters.

—It can give you *immediate* reactions, the results of the *immediate* pooling of ideas. Ideas that can be aired and discussed *at one time* by all concerned.

—It can reduce tensions to a minimum and resolve violently conflicting points of view by bringing them out into the open where they can be talked about.

—*Most important*, by drawing on the thinking of many people, it can solve problems, produce decisions, and materially reduce the chance of being wrong.

There has been much talk about the meeting producing little and wasting good time. When you hear this, just ask, "Have you a better system?"

Those who condemn the meeting are frequently those who most misuse it!

|||| BEFORE THE TALKING BEGINS

The productive meeting is built on a foundation which is laid long before the members take their places. The meeting that operates effectively to develop an idea or solve a problem is set up *before the meeting* in the minds of the individuals who will attend. Careful premeeting thinking and premeeting planning are essential. It is foolish to believe that good meetings just "happen." If you want a successful meeting, you must demand preparation.

The meeting that works is the result of exacting planning by both the leader *and* the individual members.

The following chapter will describe for you some of the basic building blocks of the good meeting. It will tell you techniques to use for efficient group speaking while outlining pitfalls that plague the meeting, the most important of all management communication tools.

These ground rules begin with the first call to the meeting—the agenda.

‖‖ BEFORE THE TALKING BEGINS
—THE AGENDA

There is no need for anyone to worry about when he should send out an agenda announcing an upcoming meeting. Always send it! The agenda is an integral part of every meeting. The agenda is the first investment in a successful meeting conclusion.

You might imagine that on June 15, 1215, a handful of noblemen and a certain Englishman named King John could have received the following agenda:

Time of meeting —June 15
Place of meeting—Field of Runnymede

Subject   —Magna Charta
Who will attend —The Barons of England
                   and King John
Goal   —Justice

This agenda was designed to set forth exactly the purpose, time, members, and goals of a meeting which would lay the foundation of Western justice and law.

This agenda naturally wasn't sent, but the form is right and will work for us today.

You can check history to find that the meeting on the field called Runnymede was a resounding success—at least if you happened to be on the side of the Barons! One good reason for the success was that everyone knew exactly *where* the subject of the meeting stood, and exactly the *goal* they wanted to reach.

More business meetings would succeed if this were also the case.

The simple, direct, well-drawn-up agenda helps guarantee this success by performing the following vital meeting functions:

1. It forces the conference-caller to present a clearly defined *problem* to be solved, and a *goal* to be reached.
2. It *reviews* the current position of the problem and brings everyone together to the meeting with a relatively *equal understanding* of the background and importance of the subject.
3. It gives all concerned a chance to think things out, a chance to develop a point of view, *and* time to gather facts to support this position.
4. The agenda demands a clearly stated estimate of how much time the meeting will take. It helps those who must be present to adjust the schedule of their busy day.
5. By stating who will be present, it helps lay out for each attending member just what points of view and opposition will be aired and what *he* must do to have his position seriously considered.

6. It serves to reduce the number of unnecessary meetings by placing the burden for calling the meeting squarely on the leader, and getting it down on paper!

In your company, in any company, an agenda is not a luxury; it is a necessity. For a better meeting, try it!

Next time you call a meeting, send out an agenda like this:

> Date—June 1, 1968
> From—Jim Fuller

Date of meeting—June 4

Place of meeting—Room 625

Subject—Product X packaging

Estimated length of meeting—1 hour

Who will attend—Anders, Murphy, Stimson, Christopher

Background of subject—Production has reported that the new package is now available.

Present position of subject—Brand man-

agement feels the design is confusing
on the shelf.

Goal of meeting—To reach complete
agreement on package and design.

Robert Burns, the Scottish poet, said that the
best laid plans of mice and men often go awry.
This may be true, but as far as we know mice don't
have to worry about meetings!

As for the men, the better the meeting plans are
laid, the less chance of getting off the track. That's
what the agenda is for.

Any agenda will work best for you in its shortest
possible form. Make every effort to keep each sec-
tion down to two sentences. The agenda that is too
long defeats its purpose.

Remember, the agenda is the first opportunity for
the meeting-caller to set a brisk tone for the meeting
to follow. If the agenda is crisp and to the point,
it may persuade the meeting and individual members to follow suit.

Do everything possible to reach *all* the members
you plan to call with the agenda at least 24 hours

before the meeting time. This will allow the members to review thoughtfully the subject to be discussed. It will allow them time to develop a point of view. It will, in addition, allow them time to support this point of view intelligently.

When you give your meeting members ample notice, you help to keep your meetings in the area of the intellect and of logical face-to-face discussion, and out of the realm of the emotions. When you do this the chances will be greater that you will reach an intelligent and logical decision.

One executive has said, "If people were forced to send out agendas, it would help them to decide whether the meeting should be called at all."

He was pointing up the known fact that a company policy of *always* sending out an agenda for a meeting will *definitely* reduce the number of unnecessary ones!

Want proof? Try it!

||| LOCATION AND SEATING FOR

THE WORKING CONFERENCE

Where you are and how you are seated will have a definite effect on the final results of your meeting. Poor lighting can make a key member irritable. A noisy room can provide just enough distraction to make agreement impossible. Bad ventilation is an excellent stimulant for conference-napping.

George Bernard Shaw said a nap was something you took when you listened to scientific lectures. It is also something you take when you sit in a poorly lit, close, badly arranged meeting room.

We try to play tennis on a firmly rolled clay

24

court. We look forward to a game of golf on a well-tended green fairway. We know that if the court and fairway are in good shape we tend to play better. Perhaps the incentive is greater.

It is natural that meeting members talk better in a well-set-up meeting room. When you think of the time spent there, it's easy to see how the comfort you gain for the participants will pay out in pleasantly arrived at, productive decisions.

Above all, the wise leader pays particular attention to the seating of the members of the meeting. He knows that conflicts can be set up *before* the talking starts.

Remember, as the meeting members come into the room and take their places, they are thinking about the meeting, the problem, and the others present. This thinking can be easily conditioned in a negative or argumentative way by poor seating arrangements and surroundings.

The leader *must* take advantage of every opportunity to promote working together, to stimulate the trading of ideas and the understanding of different points of view. It is from this understanding that the final decision will be formed.

For instance: If the members of one department, group, or school of thought are lined up on one side of the table, and their opponents are on the other, what could be more natural than a battle? The sides have already been drawn up for a fight. All that is needed is for the meeting to begin and for someone to throw out the challenge! You can be sure it won't be long in coming.

This "dividing up of sides" type of seating stresses conflict and disagreement. There's strength in numbers, and any united front will promote rigidness and intrenchment in preconceived ideas. All too often the wrong kind!

The secret ingredient of the meeting situation is coöperation.

Suggestion: Break up groups that tend to form into obstruction units. When people are separated physically, they naturally tend to think separately. And individual thinking can only help to lead to the right solutions.

Suggestion: Try to keep hostile members apart. The meeting table is not designed for the airing of personal conflicts. Distance will definitely make the hearts of two opposites grow fonder! The space between argumentative members will do much to assist the leader to exert control.

Suggestion: Use a wide, centrally placed table for your meetings. Meetings held in close, cramped rooms with the members jammed together around narrow tables would make for unpleasant conversation, let alone decision-making. Tension is built by closed-in and uncomfortable meeting rooms, and tension is without a doubt the prime breeder of conflict.

Suggestion: Make every effort to hold your meetings in the place *designed* for them—the meeting room. Not only is the meeting room set up for meetings, i.e., pencils, paper, space, etc., it also gives the group a feeling of coming together for a specific purpose, at a specific time, to solve a specific problem. This feeling creates an atmosphere of urgency and seriousness which definitely helps direct the meeting to a successful conclusion.

In addition, "meeting room meetings" avoid the looseness and lack of preparation common in the "come into my office" type of meeting.

Suggestion: Avoid the use of looooong, narrow tables that make it impossible for one member to see the other, and that place the leader out in left field. Such a seating arrangement makes it almost impossible for the leader to exert the control needed for the direct, efficient meeting. The wisdom of this suggestion will come through most clearly to those who have spent an hour or so trying to peer through an interlocking maze of heads in an effort to see where the voice is coming from!

Suggestion: The leader should place himself in a central position in order to control the meeting most effectively. This position may be at the head of the table, it may be on the side. This will be determined basically by the size of the meeting. Rule of thumb: if there are more than 12 members, sit in the center on the side. It will allow you to *face* more of your group.

Don't think of your taking of the central spot

as a presumptuous move. The leader *must* take physical as well as verbal control of the meeting if the group is to talk together effectively. If the leader sits off to one side inconspicuously, the group will treat his efforts to control with contempt.

Suggestion: See that your meeting room is well aired and well lighted. Thousands of businessmen will walk out of hundreds of dimly lighted, poorly ventilated rooms this coming week. The majority of them will have to walk back again to solve the same problems again! Give your meeting every chance of success. The members will recognize your efforts and will contribute generously.

Think of the above suggestions just five minutes before your next meeting. The conference will be better for having done so.

Avoid the following seating plans in setting up a meeting. They underline conflict, encourage disunity, make good leadershp almost impossible.

These seating plans represent mistakes made by thousands of leaders in thousands of meetings every day. They are a major barrier to the effective face-to-face trading of ideas.

These seating plans can work only one way . . . against you!

Table Too Narrow

Poor Leader Visibility

Avoid seating like this—it will build tension and stress conflict and dissension.

Conflict of Groups

Poor Leader Position

The following arrangements for seating take advantage of the physical setup of the table and kindle a desire in the group to work together. They will stimulate free exchange, stress coöperation, and move you rapidly to your solutions.

The good meeting is a result of good planning. The seating of the members is the leader's first opportunity to point out this careful planning to the group.

Here is one example of seating that will work.

Good Visibility—Good Leadership Position

These additional seating arrangements accent the positive. They make the leader's job much, much easier!

Excellent Visibility Promotes Flow of Ideas

Leadership Position for Larger Meetings

IIII ON THE SIZE OF THE MEETINGS

John M. McCaffery, former President of International Harvester, is reported to have commented on the problem of human relations in business by saying, "The biggest problem with industry is that it is full of people."

He could have been referring to the problem of meetings as well!

There can be no doubt that one of the major troubles with many meetings is that they are too full of people . . . people who need not, who should not be sitting around the already crowded meeting table.

All too often, people are called to meetings that do *not* require their presence. This waste of time and talent costs business and industry untold thousands of dollars a day in the misdirected time of valuable personnel. Over and over you hear the plea, "Keep the number of people at your meetings down." The suggestions that follow are designed to help you do just that!

But there is an even more serious result of too many people at your meetings. That is the confusion this overstaffing injects into this problem-solving situation.

Look at it this way. The perceptive meeting member recognizes the poor planning and waste of time inherent in the top-heavy group. He resents it and this resentment can only complicate the path from problem to solution.

And then there's the extra member himself. What does he feel? Remember, everyone invited to a meeting senses he must make a contribution. The extra meeting member, who is very likely only casually acquainted with the subject being discussed, is in an awkward spot. You'll get no sympathy from him! Sure, he'll try to throw something out to the group, but remember that his "forced" offering may well do nothing but cloud the issue. Equally important, it may double the length of your meeting.

Calling just the right people to your meetings demands careful evaluation. You may find that it demands more than this . . . it may promote another look at the setup of your various departments to determine who the spokesmen should be and what authority each must have. Any way you look at it, calling just the necessary meeting members will save time and money!

Use the following ideas as a guide to the size of your meetings:

1. *Make every effort to limit the number at your meetings to 15.* Any larger meeting is very difficult to control. The leader finds the larger meeting unwieldy, difficult to lead through the steps necessary in the successful group examination and solution of a problem. Since the purpose of the meeting is to draw on the thinking of all present, it is obvious that the large meeting makes forward progress slow.

2. *Limit the representatives from each*

department. Discourage the tendency of a department manager *plus* several assistants sitting in on your meetings. This doubling up in meetings is a common practice in most companies. It is costly, unwieldy, and unnecessary. It is one more barrier to direct, efficient decisions. One department representative is enough—don't have two!

Make this point diplomatically to your most frequent meeting members as soon as you get a chance. It's possible it has not occurred to them.

3. *Urge each department representative to bring the point of view of his department.* This is one of the reasons the *complete* agenda is so very important. When the people to be present at your meeting have a clear picture of the problem to be discussed, they can easily hold a premeeting discussion *within* their own departments. This

improves the chance that they will have a firm point of view to give at your meeting. This will result in contributions that are definite, direct, and constructive.

4. *Be sure the representative of each department has the authority to make the decision for his department.* No meeting can succeed if the members do not have the decision-making authority. The meeting is basically a decision-making tool. It is designed to mold facts, ideas, points of view, etc., into a firm solution. It is *only* a tool, however. It can be completely frustrated by indecisive members!

Again, examine your organization carefully to see if this weak link exists in the chain of decision-making activity.

NOTE: If you must carry the findings of this meeting to other members of your department, *say so!* This statement of policy or position is usually made in the *solution step* (see p. 116) of your meeting. Too often a meeting member who cannot give a final department position appears to the other members to be stalling. He probably has assumed that the others understood his intention.

This is a dangerous assumption—it's very misleading to others—and it wastes valuable time!

There will be times, obviously, when it will be impossible to live by the first suggestion, to limit the size of your meetings to 15 members. When the larger meeting is demanded by the situation, consider the following ideas:

    1. The "learning-conference" can be expanded to over 15 members more easily than the "decision-making meeting." The purpose of the learning or training conference is just what the name states . . . to pass and examine information. The size of the meeting is of less importance here. Here the forward progress of the meeting is not as vital as the presenting of ideas.

2. The decision-making meeting must do more than bring out ideas; it must mold them into decisions. The smaller conference obviously does this better.

3. If you must have a *very large* decision-making group (25 and up), you should make adjustment to the situation. Break the group down into small units (6 is a good size). Make each unit examine the problem and come to a decision. Then have each unit send a representative to a final meeting group. Let the others involved listen in as audience.

This so called 'buzz technique' breaks an unwieldy mass down into compact working meetings. If this fits your needs, try it. You'll find it works!

IIII HOW LONG SHOULD THE MEETING BE?

Standing on a hill just before the battle of Austerlitz, which was to make him the conqueror of Europe, Napoleon ordered a regiment on his left flank to be brought up. He was told hesitantly by an aide that this move would take time. His answer was sharp and to the point.

"Go, sir, gallop, and don't forget that the *world* was made in six days. You can ask me for anything you like, *except* time!"

All people value time highly. They resent it when it is wasted or misused. The meeting member feels this emotion very strongly. He wants to see time used efficiently and fully.

It's impossible to set a standard time limit for *all* meetings. Naturally, this must be determined by the subject at hand. However, we can lay some guiding ground rules. The most effective meetings last no longer than one and a half hours. Longer meetings fall off badly in productiveness. In fact, they set up definite barriers to decisions. Clear thinking falters as the clock goes round, and in turn, emotions take over. Weariness breeds dissension and contrariness.

Short, single problems *can* be solved in less than an hour. This is a goal to shoot for! Too often the reason meetings last longer is not because of the subject, but because the people examining it are not moving directly down the path from problem to solution. Here the leader must see the group directs full attention to the major question and does not waste time on tangential details.

The real need today is for the crisp conference of the 20-minute variety. *This* is the meeting all business is waiting for. This is the meeting this book is designed to promote!

One of the most gratifying meetings this author ever attended was opened by the leader like this:

"The problem we have to look at today is a difficult one. It is a vital one for our company because it is right at the core of our production operation. Whatever changes may be made will have broad and immediate effects on us all. *I think we can solve it in 30 minutes!*"

And it was solved. In 30 minutes!

From a straight dollars-and-cents basis, nothing reflects more credit on the meeting members and the leader than the solving of an important problem in a short time. Too many people erroneously equate the important problem with the *long,* drawn-out meeting. They seem to believe the length of the meeting shows a respect for the seriousness of the question to be resolved. This is, of course, absurd. Naturally, business men recognize the importance of the ideas they talk about. There is no need for an artificial relationship between the importance of the subject and the time spent on it.

The responsibility of time rests squarely with the leader. Don't allow meeting members to circle around the problem like hungry lions wary of the hidden hunter. If you sense a hesitancy among the members born of a feeling of the importance of the problem, take over quickly! Drive right at the heart of the matter. Make the members take hold. Force the group to face up squarely to the problem. Urge them to analyze and decide on a solution.

It would be good to follow Ben Franklin's advice:

"Dost thou love life? Then do not squander time, for that is the stuff life is made of."

The expressed desire for brevity made by the leader in a meeting is valuable bait for future successful *short* meetings!

|||| FOUR COMMON TYPES OF BUSINESS MEETINGS

The type of business meeting to be used in any situation is, of course, determined by the goal of the meeting itself. What do you want to get done? Do you want to gather facts from many sources to give someone a better understanding of a problem? Do you want to train new personnel or employees who are moving into a new job area? Do you want to come up with a new idea, a new method of production, a new advertising theme? Or do you want to make a decision or establish operating policy?

There is a meeting type designed to do each of these in the most direct, simplest, and most successful way.

Basically, the differences in each type are differences in the form of leadership—differences in the degree of control exerted over the meeting members. Again, the amount of control or freedom needed by the discussing members is determined by what the group and the leader are trying to accomplish.

Here are the four types of meetings most widely and successfully used in business today:

1. The Report Meeting
2. The Decision-Making Meeting
3. The Development or Creative Meeting
4. The Learning or Training Meeting

Each of the above types fulfills a need in group communication. It is vitally important to understand the advantages and restrictions of each. The businessman is a workman; like all workmen he depends heavily on the tools at his command.

The following describes briefly each type of meeting and sets forth its specific application.

The Report Meeting. An authoritarian conference guided by the strong direction of the leader. Designed for the rapid and direct presentation of reports by the

individual members, this type of meeting
is unproductive for the creative development of ideas, or for coöperative decision-
making. (See pp. 45-49 for a full discussion of the report meeting.)

The Decision-Making Meeting. This
type is the most used and probably the
most productive meeting in business
today. It is specifically designed to draw
together the thinking of the various working parts of an organization and to form
this thinking into a decision. This type
meeting should be used by all policy-
making and problem-solving groups. (See
pp. 49-55 for a full discussion.)

The Development or Creative Meeting.
This type is particularly well suited to
groups called upon to create new ideas or
to develop and expand as yet undefined
concepts, strategies, theories, etc. It operates best with a minimum of control from
the leader. It is extremely productive
when its free-flowing form is applied to

creative problems. This meeting in its extreme form has been referred to in business as "brain-storming." (See pp. 55-60 for discussion.)

The Learning or Training Meeting. The problem of training is a constant one with all organizations. Basic to this problem is the passing of information in the simplest, most easily understood form. Business and industry have found that the training meeting does this better than any other tested method. It has several obvious advantages. It is less rigid than the usual formal presentation of information. It allows the members to relax and get to know one another. It allows those who are learning to dig more deeply into those areas they feel are important and which will help them most. It allows ample time for the free discussion of pertinent questions and answers.

It is by *far* the best way business has found to train empolyees! (See pp. 61-

68 for a full discussion of the learning or training meeting.)

THE REPORT MEETING

In the Middle Ages the alchemists were all searching feverishly for the lodestone, the magical element that would turn lead into gold. Kings and paupers in the dead of night bent over violently boiling cauldrons, all hoping to find this great treasure.

Needless to say, they never did.

Today's businessman has been more successful—in a different way!

There is a vast supply of gold to be found in business in reducing the time and error that goes with the passing of information. In this case the lodestone of the businessman is the report meeting —if it is used correctly.

The report meeting is just what the name implies. It is a meeting designed for the direct presentation of information.

The report meeting is *not* a democratic committee.

It is not a free-wheeling creative group called together for the development of bright, new ideas. It is not a discussion group for the practice of mental gymnastics!

If it is *not* these things, what *is* it?

It is an autocratic and authoritarian meeting designed for passing concise, fully-developed information with tight control exerted by the leader in order to operate in minimum time. It sounds like this:

"Jim, will you give us the information on the production timetable?"

"Andy, what can we expect in the way of distribution in the southwest district?"

"Bill, what are our shipments in Dallas?"

The report meeting is a valuable tool to any organization. It offers the following advantages:

1. It is an excellent way of gathering factual information from a group of specialists.

2. It is a sure, direct method of getting information to top executives who *must* be kept up to date, but who are not actively working on this specific project.

3. It is a positive way of passing informa-

tion with equal understanding to all concerned, since the emphasis, tone, and urgency of the subject will be received by all present. The chance of equal understanding is therefore greater

4. It reduces the danger of misunderstanding. Questions can be asked. Any confusion or wrong personal interpretation can be exposed and corrected early.

5. It eliminates, or at least reduces the sending of many, many, many memos!

It is truly said that business gets bigger, but our ability to "get ideas around" stays the same size!

Here's how to use the report meeting and to make it work for you and your company.

Be sure you give speakers sufficient time to prepare for their reports. 24 hours if possible!

Be specific as to the theme of the meeting. Everyone must be working in the *same* direction, to the *same* goal, and thinking of details on the *same* subject.

Be sure each member knows *exactly* the area he is responsible for.

Urge that the reports be *spoken,* not read. Notes, of course, can be used.

As leader, make a clear, *short* opening statement. State the goal . . . and stress *time*!

Control the meeting firmly. Do not allow unnecessary discussion.

Make members report *on their feet.* It usually makes for better preparation.

Request brief statements of fact, opinion, decision. Discourage long-winded elaboration.

Suggest the use of visuals. The chart, pictograph, and diagram promote directness and clarity.

At the end of the meeting state the next action to be taken.

Use the report meeting. It has a vital role to play in your company.

THE DECISION-MAKING MEETING

Napoleon was once asked what troops he preferred. "Simple," he answered. "The victorious ones."

That's the kind of meetings executives like, too. The ones that do the job they are called for. The meetings that come to decisions!

This demands a discussion of the most used, most abused meeting type in business—the decision-making meeting.

Decisions are the manufactured product of the raw materials of facts, ideas, theories, and opinions. They are the fuel of today's successful business and industrial organization. There can be no cut-back in decisions. They are an *absolute* require-ment for *every* company. Every business executive makes dozens of them every working day. Decisions —they're his job!

The decision-making meeting is one answer to the increased demand placed on the businessman. It is being used by more and more busy executives to help them ration their time and to do their job better. Business today is too complex; too big for all daily decisions to be made by one man alone. He finds he must call more and more on the thinking of the people around him. It is still possible to have the complete business autocrat, but think of the loss of the talented thinking of so *many* valuable people that make up the average company!

The decision-making meeting must justify its name. It must produce the answers to questions, produce decisions. It is aimed at solving specific problems or establishing operating policy. It is designed to draw out the thinking of informed indi-viduals and to mold this thinking into a final course of action.

The decision-making meeting produces conclusions built on facts. These facts are available within the group and a decision can only be made when these facts have been fully presented. The facts must come out! When these building blocks are not available, either because of poor preparation, reluctance on the part of the members to speak up, or a head-long rushing to decisions, the meeting will very likely fail.

Your decision-making meeting group must understand the meeting form to make it do the job it can do well.

Too many attempts have been made to equate the ideas of democracy and equality with the meeting situation. This is done in all good faith, since the discussion in its pure form is perhaps the most democratic of all speech techniques. Books outlining the discussion technique constantly underlined that all members must have equal opportunity to present their ideas.

This is admirable. But don't mistake the business meeting for a "Great Books" discussion group. Or get the idea that the rules for the town meeting hold true for an industrial policy-forming board. If you do you are whistling in the dark!

Business meetings *must* run on a close schedule. Therefore discussion *is* frequently curtailed. The secret is to get the important ideas aired. All people in the business meeting are *not* equal. The important thing is to see that the idea of the junior executive *is* presented—and given the examination it deserves. These goals can be guaranteed by only one person—the leader.

The decision-making meeting demands much of the leader. He must see that all the necessary information is presented. He must see that everyone who has an important contribution to make gets the chance. He must see that the meeting is self-contained; that an agreement or compromise is reached *in* the meeting. Not in the hallway later on in the day! He must keep the meeting on the track, allow for discussion of all points of view, and, at the same time, hold to a business timetable.

This is not easy. Perhaps leading a decision-making meeting is the most difficult job a businessman is asked to do. He must, however, learn to do it, and learn it well. He holds the key to the success-ful passing of information in business today.

The decision-making meeting calls for a firm hand and an accurately directed leadership. This guidance will determine the success of the group in reaching a decision. The free-flowing, freely con-trolled development or creative meeting form will not work here.

To set the pattern, the leader must:

1. Open the meeting with a clear, brief, direct statement of the problem to be examined.

2. Direct the meeting in an examination of the background of the problem, the goals to be reached, and possible solutions. Make the group decide how the solutions can be applied.

3. Make sharp, to the point summaries to nail down agreements, disagreements, and compromises.

4. Keep the meeting on the track. Dis-courage irrelevant chatter.

5. Sum up the decisions reached and

state clearly the next steps to be taken.

6. Watch the time *carefully*!

The leader is the navigator in the decision-making group. He keeps the meeting right on target.

Leader

The good leader has been accurately described as an individual who can set up a situation which other people can handle without trouble. In other words, good leadership avoids meeting snarls and clears the way for the members to reach an easy decision.

The accompanying diagram shows the flow of ideas from the members of the group and the degree of control exerted by the leader in the decision-making meeting.

In this type of meeting the information is presented freely by all present and is guided by the comments, clarifications, restatements, and summaries of the leader.

Next time you are a member of the decision-making meeting, sit back for a moment and evaluate. See if the meeting is doing the job it was designed for—drawing on the thinking of the group and heading for a decision.

(For a full discussion of the leader's job, see pp. 69-105.)

THE CREATIVE OR DEVELOPMENT MEETING

The decision-making meeting is designed to resolve problems, establish policy, and direct action toward a determined meeting decision. The decisions reached in this type of meeting are the end result of a careful blending and meshing of the facts, figures, and ideas presented by the group.

The goal of the creative meeting is different. The building materials in this meeting are the imaginative, fertile ideas so vital to the growth and development of every organization.

Let's look closely at the creative meeting and find out how it works!

The development meeting can be best used in business as a means of dealing with the evaluation and discussion of as yet unformed *new* ideas.

This type of meeting is guided under what may be called the "free-flowing" form. This guidance requires the minimum of control from the leader and offers broad leeway to the members of the group to reach out for the discovery, development, and application of original ideas and concepts.

The development meeting is a natural for advertising creative groups, new product development teams, product merchandising departments.

The leader of the development meeting has a difficult job. His group is dealing with spontaneous and highly productive material. He must guide just enough to give this material form and permanence.

Of necessity, his guidance must be flexible and fluid.

Ideas are a valuable and volatile substance. They are hard to find, more difficult to develop. They frequently seem to defy communication to others. They are, of course, the "stuff" that business is made of; the raw materials of tomorrow's production.

The creative or development meeting is designed to handle this "hot" material.

Everyone recognizes the growing need in business and industry for men to work together in the joint development of new products, design of new packaging, and discovery of new production methods.

This calls for better communication of ideas between all these varied groups!

The research engineer must review his plans with company management. The advertising manager must discuss advertising plans with the marketing men. The chemist must know what the man at the next table is working on. All these activities call for the joining of the developmental abilities of the entire company. Individual departments can no longer "go it alone."

The development meeting does not strike out for

immediate solutions. It is better suited to nourish and nurture an idea, an idea that did not exist earlier.

The goal is the developed idea. An idea created by a group of people *thinking aloud* together.

The creative or development meeting demands the unlimited efforts of *all* members present. The material must be presented, examined, qualified, added to, weighed, and finally molded into a completed concept or idea. This is a big order for the meeting members. It is even a bigger one for the leader.

The following guides will help to make your next creative meeting more productive.

1. As leader, see that the subject to be discussed is clearly stated for the group. Make it brief and to the point.
2. Draw out individual contributions. Encourage direct simple language. Discourage jargon!
3. Listen patiently and carefully to all offerings. Evaluate whether a sugges-

tion applies to the subject at hand. If not, make your next comment draw the discussion gently back. In this meeting, *too* much control will inhibit the group.

4. Clarify your own and other contributions by using examples, illustrations, comparisons, etc. The most difficult idea becomes easy to understand when contrasted or compared to something with which we are all familiar.

5. Constantly stress the positive. Keep indicating to the group that this is a meeting that *can* and *will* turn up an idea of value.

The leader's main job in this type of meeting is to govern as little as possible and yet keep the meeting moving along the main line.

The result will be the original thinking of creative people, which is the fuel of today's business and industry.

The leader of the creative meeting must learn

how to keep the information flowing into the hands of the members present. He must also channel the direction of this information. This delicate balance is diagramed in the accompanying illustration.

Leader

This indicates the freedom the good leader allows in the development meeting. The keynote: *guidance* but not rigid *control*.

THE LEARNING OR TRAINING MEETING

"Interesting, but what good is it?" said a skeptical man watching the ascent of the first balloon.

"What good is a new-born baby?" was Benjamin Franklin's piercing reply.

The secret, which our short-sighted friend did not live long enough to learn, is application. The application of a new idea or technique to a specific and practical use.

Big organizations have learned that the meeting is not only a place to hammer out decisions. They have learned it is also a valuable training tool, a means to review methods based on the experience of old hands, and a way to indoctrinate new personnel.

There are several definite advantages to the training meeting as a means to better personnel development.

Let's see what the "training table" can do!

    1. The learning meeting reduces the formality always present when new and senior members of a company come together. It stimulates a freer

and therefore more valuable exchange of information.

2. Trainees have the opportunity of drawing on the thinking of *several* specialists in the same meeting. They can hear the evaluation of ideas by different meeting members which helps them gain a broader background on the subject.

3. The learning members can dig deeply into areas they think will help *them* most, simply by asking questions. Questions are easier to ask around the meeting table than they would be in a formal lecture presentation.

4. The learning meeting is a training tool that lets the trainee "run with the ball" himself. Many times trainees will find they can analyze the problems under discussion by themselves. This is a great stimulant. Nothing is as gratifying or lasting as having come to the answer by yourself!

5. The training meeting is not only a good method of presenting ideas to new personnel, it also helps them develop an ease of talking together. This is perhaps as important as the original training goal. Their ability to talk together will be of vital importance to the company and may, more than anything else, determine their own business future.

6. The training meeting sets a pattern for working together and coming to an agreed-upon group decision. It teaches the need for understanding and diplomacy. It teaches the need to listen to the fellow across the table, and the need for proof if you want him to accept your point. It teaches trainees to deal in facts and to avoid emotion in talking together.

   Above all, it teaches that in business everything is *not* black and white. That compromise is an honorable ap-

proach. Frequently it is the only logical way to move an idea forward!

All over the world the training meeting is being
used to do a job it can do better than any other
method: to teach, train, pass out, sift, and evaluate
ideas.

The job of the leader of the training meeting is
relatively simple—as long as he understands just
what he is trying to do.

Above all, remember the training meeting is not
designed to make decisions. Nor is it directed to
create new or original ideas. The purpose of this
meeting type is to set up an effective training or
learning climate for the passing and discussing of
information.

The leader can do this best by:

1. Clearly stating the subject to be discussed. If you wish to restrict the scope
   of the review, be sure you say so.
   Realize that wandering off the subject
   will be one of the major problems
   you will have to control.

2. Turning to one of the meeting mem-

bers and posing a definite question—
one that cannot be answered with a
"yes" or "no." This is the best way to
break the ice and to strike out into
the discussion.

3. Moving back into the discussion after
the first couple of contributions if there
is any doubt that the meeting is moving in the right direction. The first remarks are extremely important in the
training meeting. Chances are that you
are dealing with inexperienced con-
ferees, and a wrong start can badly
divert the meeting.

4. Spotlighting important contributions
by expressing your interest. Say,
"That's a very important point, John.
How do you feel it effects our production?"

5. Making frequent summaries to keep
the meeting on the track.

6. Trying to stay out of the discussion
as much as possible. Work as a foil;

stimulate questions, ask for clarifications, make comparisons. Work as a
catalyst, an element which is not part
of the whole but which acts to keep
things in action, working. If authority
is needed, try to get one of the senior
meeting members to take over the job.

7. Drawing reluctant meeting members
   into the discussion. Get everyone to
   join in. One of the benefits of the training meeting is that the individual
   members not only get to know each
   other personally, they get to know each
   other's thinking as well.

8. Making a final summary of the discussion. Again, clearly state the purpose of the meeting. Make it clear that
   the goal of the meeting *was* accom-
   plished. That the meeting was not
   called to solve a problem, but to discuss a particular subject so that all
   would understand it better. Too often
   members of a training meeting feel

the meeting was a failure because a decision was not reached. Set this straight!

The success of the training or learning meeting depends heavily on the ability of the group to roam freely through a subject and to look at it from all sides. This calls for minimum control—maximum guidance—maximum flow of ideas.

This type of meeting can be applied quickly and easily to modern business and industry. Like all other speech-communication forms, it demands that secret ingredient to which many *truly* great men admit they owe success: "Practice. Practice. Practice."

Leadership

‖‖ SUCCESSFUL LEADERSHIP

"Nothing astonishes men so much as common sense and plain dealing."
—Ralph Waldo Emerson

The core of the successful meeting is the man who combines the virtues set forth by Mr. Emerson. This *is* the leader. His job is to lead.

The leaders of today's business meetings do not just happen. They must *learn* to handle the complex job of resolving problems, controlling emotions and passing information . . . and learn to do these accurately and expediently.

This is a job for specialists—specialists in a job that is never the same twice. The meeting leader must always remain flexible to the needs and demands of each specific meeting and adjust to those needs with ease and authority.

The leader is like the hub of a working gear. He is the center around which all else revolves. He has to be alert to any change of pace. He must move faster to adjust to changes than any other part of the mechanism. Nevertheless, it is the members who provide the drive. The leader is never more than the guide.

There is no doubt that more than anyone else, the leader is responsible for the successful meeting. He is also responsible for most failures.

The able leader is indispensable!

During a lull in the midst of street fighting in the Franco-Prussian War, a young man leaned out of a doorway to shout to a friend who was following about twenty yards behind a mob.

"Where's the mob headed?"

"To the barricades."

"Why are you following?"

"I've got to!"

"Why?"

"Because I'm their leader!"

This, unfortunately, is the kind of leadership too many meetings also get, and it is not the leadership that produces successful, time-saving, productive, decisive meetings. In the meeting room, the leader is *never* the follower. This is a basic, all inclusive, eternal rule.

Suggestion: Make it clear to your meeting members, and to your whole organization, just what the leader is supposed to do. *He is supposed to lead. He* is the one responsible for the direction, temper, pace, and final decisions reached by the group. This may take some education. People just naturally feel they shouldn't appear to be too autocratic. The plain fact that the leader *must* take his position behind the wheel is the most important concept for meeting members and prospective leaders to learn.

The leader has a clearly defined status:

1. He is not just another member.
2. He is *supposed* to have more authority than anyone else in the meeting. This is not tyranny!
3. He must be more conscious of time and

the effectiveness of the meeting than
anyone else.

After all, the leader is responsible to the other
members and to himself for the productiveness of
the meeting.

The meeting is an investment in time. It must be
made to pay out!

|||| LEADERSHIP IN OPENING
THE MEETING

Just 2000 years ago the most famous writer in the all-powerful Roman Empire set down a valuable rule of thumb. He stated:

"He who has made a good beginning has half the deed done."

The meeting leader would do well to heed this advice of Cicero. The opening of the meeting is like a horse race, or the painter first putting the brush to the blank canvas. Like the horse race, a bad start almost eliminates any chance of a win. Like the painting, the first stroke sets the direction of what will follow.

With the meeting, the beginning is crucial.

Follow these rules in opening *your* meeting to take advantage of every chance of success.

Rule one: *Start on time!* Ask any frequent meeting member how many meetings start promptly as scheduled. This is probably the most violated of all meeting rules. And, paradoxically, the easiest rule for the leader to enforce. He has full responsibility and control over the opening of the meeting. Too often you hear this:

"Well, it's time to start, but Bill Carson isn't here. We'd better wait a few minutes."

Don't do it! Think of all the people who *are* there! If you wait for Carson, at the next meeting all the rest will be late. The leader who begins the meeting promptly will be immediately recognized and respected. He will stand out—there are so few like him!

If you do nothing else to improve your meetings, this will be a *big* step. Remember, to start on time means you have a better chance to *end* on time.

Set the standard. There will be lots of followers!

Rule two: *State the purpose of the meeting clearly.* You have set down in your agenda the sub-

ject and purpose of your meeting. Remember, however, that this agenda is probably at least 24 hours
old. Many pieces of paper have passed over the
meeting member's desks in the meantime. A restatement is *essential*. This will lead the members right
up to the problem, and gently nudge them in. Your
oral presentation will help to clearly define the
problem for all present. It can easily clear up any
last-minute confusions.

Above all, your restatement will give the subject
the immediacy and urgency it deserves!

Rule three: *State your ideas positively*. Nothing
succeeds like success. Nothing suggests success like
the opening remarks that clearly say that success is
possible. The tone of your remarks will immediately
set the stage and direction of those that will follow.
Point out the importance of the problem. State the
implications and effects of the decisions that will
be made at *this* meeting. Show that the meeting is
worth while, and give the members something to
shoot for. *Don't be negative!*

Too often you hear opening remarks like this:
"This is a difficult problem. A lot of people have

looked at it, and it <u>hasn't been solved yet.</u> I <u>doubt</u> <u>whether we can</u> do anything about it. But, I <u>guess</u> <u>we should look at it,</u> and <u>try to work it out.</u>"

The underlined words are the kind that will guarantee the failure of *any* meeting.

<u>difficult problem</u>—what isn't! Why underline the point? The group will determine how difficult it is.

<u>lot of people</u>—they haven't been able to work it out. Implies this group will fail too.

<u>hasn't been solved yet</u>—naturally! If it had, this meeting wouldn't have been necessary. This will do nothing but make solution harder.

<u>doubt whether we can</u>—what can be more negative? Makes this meeting totally unnecessary.

<u>guess we should look at it</u>—another wasted comment. Of course you should look at it. That's why you're there!

<u>try to work it out</u>—translation: "We'll make an attempt to solve the problem, but chances are we'll fail." This cer-

tainly won't make the members strike
out boldly for solutions.

Give the group a fair shake. Let them know that
this meeting has a good chance to solve *this* problem.
If this isn't so, there's no reason for them to give up
their valuable time.

Rule four: *Use words that make your ideas sound
interesting.* The crispness and vitality of your opening remarks will set the tone and pace of the entire
meeting. Frame your ideas in colorful phrases. For
instance, this is the type of statement that smothers
meetings:

"We should try to appraise the possibilities of
purveying the meat currently in inventory."

Try this:

"Gentlemen, this is a problem we *must* resolve.
The meat is on the hooks. We've got to sell it or
smell it!"

Stimulation is essential to success at this point of
the meeting. Remember, the meeting members are
very likely tired. They may be thinking of some
other problem. This may be their fifth meeting of the
day. The leader must do more than just present the
facts of the problem. He must revitalize and stimu-

late them if he wants to draw on the full value of their thinking.

The leader wants to enlist the unqualified attention and effort of his group. He must use direct and unqualified words.

Rule five: *Limit your opening remarks to one and one-half minutes*. The leader's job is to present the problem to be discussed to the group clearly and fully. He must also communicate the urgency of the problem in order to move the group to action. Long-drawn-out openings take the edge off this urgency, and cause a misfire right at the beginning. Don't be like the long-winded lawyer who, after a long, dull speech, said sarcastically to the judge,

"I trust I am not unduly trespassing on the time of this court."

"My friend," returned the judge, "there is a considerable difference between trespassing on time and encroaching on eternity!"

The opening of the meeting is a time for direct talk!

Straight-forward opening remarks by the leader make his next job easier, that of leadership *during* the meeting.

‖‖ LEADERSHIP DURING THE MEETING

"The only thing needed for the triumph of evil is that good men do nothing."
—*Edmund Burke*

The only thing needed for the best-planned meeting to degenerate into chaos is for the *leader* to do nothing!

Leadership is an active force—it cannot be passive. It is a force which exerts itself to guide, direct, restrict, develop, contain, expand, elicit, repress, and generally stimulate the examining and developmental thinking of the group. The leader during the meeting is an active counselor, guide, administrator, compromiser—he is in fact all things to the meeting as they are needed.

The balance of how much and how little control the leader should exert during the meeting calls for a fine discrimination in judgment and a generous mixture of common sense. This is not a balance that can be outlined accurately in any book. It can only be gained by a clear understanding of the duties of the leader and the goals of the meeting. And by doing!

The human mind has been compared to a giant switchboard which stores and catalogues thoughts and ideas, like a massive IBM computer which has all the facts and which applies them at the appropriate moment to solve a specific question.

Like the computer, the mind responds to a particular happening and triggers a response drawn from these stored thoughts. The demand sets up the situation and the mind plugs in to form the connection.

The leader has a similar function. He sorts and catalogues the ideas presented by the meeting members. He is constantly alert to the needs of the group.

He applies information when it is needed. He maintains the connections necessary to guarantee the flow of ideas. He watches constantly for the flashing red light which warns of a conflict, a sidetrack, a misunderstanding.

Like the computer, the leader is a self-correcting guide who moves quickly within the group to adjust to changes in the meeting direction and tone.

One thing is sure . . . the job of the leader is to lead *throughout* the meeting. He cannot be a figurehead. He cannot be an announcer who comes in at the beginning and end. He is *always* the hub of the meeting wheel. He governs much or little according to the demand of the situation. *But he controls the meeting* all the way through. He knows his job is to bring the group in on the beam, and he accepts this responsibility.

There are unfortunately too few good meeting leaders. They are an extremely valuable asset to every organization. Be one!

Here are some ground rules for effective leadership:

> *Remain impartial if possible.* The

leader functions best as the sorter, sifter, clarifier, and director in the meeting. Report facts, guide the discussion, watch for conflicts and personality flare-ups. Channel the group toward possible solutions. Emotions and facts *must* mix whenever people talk face to face. However, the emotional tone of the meeting will be better, and the meeting easier to handle, if you as leader can assume a neutral position.

Suggestion: If you must present a point of view or declare a personal position, try to do it through another member of your department. Or, draw a statement of your position from one of the other meeting members.

Watch the pacing of the meeting. Keep the meeting moving. Remember, in the platform speech, it is possible to carefully time your ideas, and to keep the thoughts marching briskly along. However, in the meeting you are dealing with perhaps a dozen people, *and* there is no script!

Think of the meetings you've attended when a sudden and deadly silence has set in and everyone sat waiting for someone else to make a comment. This is an unpleasantly awkward situation, and awkwardness breeds tension! Tension is a direct road to conflict, dissension, and confusion.

Keep the ideas flowing. Once this flow flags it is difficult, often impossible, to reopen the tap. The leader must run herd on the group; keep nudging to maintain the pace.

Suggestion: Be alert to "silent periods." Move quickly to comment, question, explain, etc., the *moment* you sense this silence settling in. When the ideas slow down, so does the urgency and the ability of the group to cope with the problem.

Watch for emotional "build-ups." Meetings are made up of people, and people are made of a little bit of logic and a *lot* of emotion! These are not the ingredients of "sweetness and light." It is the leader's job to maintain order and reasonableness.

The more the discussion stays in the realm of fact, the better the chance of success. There is usually no answer to emotional conflicts.

It has been suggested that people don't want facts. This is probably true. They would rather have one good, soul-searching emotion than a dozen facts. Unfortunately, emotions don't solve problems or make rational decisions. Facts do!

Suggestion: Watch for the building of emotional tension between individuals or groups. Move in quickly to put out the fire. Change the direction of the meeting *away* from "tender" points. Use humor to lighten the air. Point out that both members *could* be right; that it all depends on where you stand, and how you look at it. When the tension has been reduced, you can turn back to a realistic look at the problem.

Pull out all background information.
There is a natural urge in human beings
to drive directly to solutions. This is high-
lighted in the meeting situation. Although
this is an admirable drive, it is some-
times like putting the motor on the boat
before the hull is finished. Decisions and
solutions can only be made on the information presented and discussed by the
group. Briefly, the major function of the
meeting technique is to get all the facts
out of the meeting members, and then to
talk about those facts. Only then can the
group hope to come to a logical and
workable solution. Make your group do
first things first. Don't let them become
solution-minded *too* soon!

Suggestion: In your opening remarks,
make it clear you want to go over the
background material *before* you try to
come up with the answers. Point out that

if this isn't done, one person alone could replace the meeting as a decision-making tool. If one of the members rushes headlong to a solution, pull him back. This is part of the leader's control duty.

Draw contributions from all members of the group. There are silent members in almost every group. The meeting situation is designed to draw on the thinking of *all* members; to call out *all* ideas and mold them into a decision.

Be sure that everyone has a chance to make his offering. Encourage the member that shows signs of meekness. Be careful, however, not to put a reluctant member on the spot. Draw him into the discussion through an area you know is familiar to him. Then dig deeper for his position on the subject at hand. This will reduce the danger of postmeeting comments, which are usually made in the hallway leaving the meeting-room, like:

"I just don't think I can go along with

the decision made in the meeting."

Or statements like this:

"That's all very well, but no one told Bill that my department just can't tool up for the job to meet that deadline."

These statements are important and pertinent. Unfortunately, they are being made at the wrong time and in the wrong place. They should have been made *in* the meeting for the enlightenment and consideration of all. Let the leader beware of these postmeeting comments! They usually mean another meeting must be called. The penalty is obvious—wasted time!

Suggestion: Be sure everyone gets in on the discussion and decisions. If you know of a particular meeting member who tends to postmeeting comments, pin him down *in* the meeting. Make him commit himself so definitely that he won't be able to say later he doesn't agree. You owe this to the group!

This is the type of leadership that can save many, many wasted hours around the meeting table.

See that only one person speaks at a time. There is no room in a meeting for a meeting within a meeting. Private discussions within the meeting group can only cause conflict and disunity. On this point, the leaders *must* be firm! Don't allow the meeting to break up into smaller discussion groups. It's the leader's job to see that each member is heard by all present. If a splinter group persists, focus the attention of the whole group on it. Like this:

"Jim and Bill seem to have come up with something. Will you tell us about it?"

They'll get the idea!

Suggestion: Exert strong enough control to "polarize" the group. Enough control to keep the group working as *one* unit, a unit working *together* to resolve the problem at hand.

Pin down opposing points of view. It would be naïve to think or expect that all the varied ideas expressed during a meeting will mesh and support one another. There are bound to be strong differences of opinion. In fact, conflict is probably vital to the development of new thinking on a problem. It stimulates members to document and prove the ideas and points of view they present.

However, this is a controlled conflict. Conflict controlled by the leader and *used* to help the group toward the ultimate solving of the subject under discussion.

Suggestion: Never disregard or attempt to hide conflicting ideas. Recognize them and point them out to the group. Bring them out into the open where they can be examined intelligently. Accept the fact that emotion is bound to enter the picture strongly, but constantly stress objectivity. Always try to strip off the emotion and examine the facts in the cold light of the meeting table. Ask the conflicting members,

"Where do you stand exactly?"

Then,

"Why do you take that position?"

And finally,

"What do *you* suggest we do?"

No ideas are held as strongly as those *not* discussed!

Stress coöperation, not conflict. Most people come to the conference with a definite point of view. Good! They know other people will disagree. Good! They are determined to *force* the others to accept their position. Bad!

This results from a misunderstanding of what the meeting is designed to do. This point calls for some well-directed teaching!

The leader must lead the group to work together. Try to present the idea that this is a problem that demands the thinking of all present. No one can go it alone in the meeting! Point out that the meeting room is not a personal battlefield. Refer to the complexity of today's business; to the growing need for specialists. Explain that the meeting is designed to draw together the thinking of all these *many* specialists. Draw out contributions by praising the group as a unit.

Suggestion: Conflict is always going to exist among people who think strongly. Take every opportunity to point out the advantages of "pooling" thinking. The feeling of coöperation will be stimulated by meetings that *work!* Successful, workable decisions are the most persuasive argument for coöperation in future meetings.

Guide the meeting from problem to solution. Move doggedly through the steps of the meeting from the presentation of materials to the final solving of the problem. Remember, the most com-

mon cause of poor meetings is lack of
direction. This places the responsibility
squarely on the head of the leader. This
is in *his* control area.

Each time a member speaks in a meeting, the direct line to the solution stands
in danger of being derailed. The wrong
emphasis, a misinterpretation of a contribution, a missed fact—any of these common happenings can send the group
slicing off the fairway. When you successfully lead a meeting, you are giving
guidance and structure to the most complex of all speaking situations.

Suggestion: Follow the "solution
wheel" pattern for problem-solving. (See
pp. 109-118.) This device is designed to
keep the meeting on the main line and to
drive it to a successful conclusion. Follow
it closely. It works!

One thing you need never doubt. Although the group may not know it, they
need all the direction they can get. When

you give it to them, they will recognize the effort. Your meetings will reflect their appreciation—in time and results.

Clarify contributions. Be sure that what is said by one member is understood by all present. One of the most common misconceptions held by people is that there is a clear line from the speaker to the listener; that the listener always understands *exactly* what is said to him. Nothing could be further from the truth.

Accept the fact that language is an inadequate method of communication. With this you must also accept that it is the only method we have and that we must strive to make it work better for us. Here's how the leader can do this in the meeting.

For instance:

Ask questions in areas that may have been missed.

"There is one question we haven't asked: 'What is the marketing potential

of this product?' Bill, what is your estimate?"

Pull out details needed to make each
offering crystal clear.

"The one point we haven't covered is
the cost of the advertising. How does this
affect the plan?"

Define words that could lead to a misinterpretation.

"Al, when you say that this idea is
'critical' to the plan, do you mean that it
wouldn't work without it?"

Ask members to elaborate.

"Jim, would you expand on that
point?"

Rephrase statements you fear might
not be clear.

"You feel that we should *not* advertise
in national magazines. Is that correct?"

Psychologists tell us that we understand best those things we know or have
experienced. Take advantage of this concept. Phrase difficult thoughts in simple,

everyday terms. Use comparisons, analogies, similes, examples, contrasts, comparisons, stories, etc. Don't be afraid of being *too* simple. You can't!

Follow Napoleon's *first* rule to his officers:

"Be clear, be clear, be clear!"

Use humor to reduce tension. It is only human nature to hold strongly to your own ideas. It's difficult to retrack and admit that someone else has reached the right conclusion while you have been wallowing in error. It's difficult for the meeting member to admit he's wrong, but it's even more difficult for him to bow out gracefully. Often a member in a meeting would like to change direction or retreat from a stand, but finds it too awkward to do so. Be alert to this situation. Give him the opportunity to revise his position without seeming to "roll over!" Again, the leader can do this job better than anyone else.

Suggestion: Try using humor to open up this common meeting roadblock. When the tension is reduced and everyone is relaxed, it's easier for the reluctant member to step down. He can then do it gracefully . . . and save face.

Make frequent summaries during the meeting. Summaries report the progress of the meeting to all present. They are a running score-card of the success of the group in attacking the problem. Summaries also serve to check on disagreements and point out to the members what conflicts demand their attention. Otherwise disagreements tend to get lost in the discussion, only to turn up at the end of the meeting, much to the dismay of all concerned. Disagreements are to be expected during the meeting, but when they are only uncovered at the end when there isn't time to handle them, all they do is frustrate the meeting members.

Suggestion: Use the "solution wheel" pattern and summarize after each step. Be alert to times in the meeting when a summary can put a thorny point away once and for all.

Summaries are like stations on a railroad. They tell you where you are, and how close you are to home.

Warning! Keep your summaries under 30 seconds. This is plenty of time to do the job. These summaries will not interrupt the flow of the meeting. They will also serve as an example to the meeting group that *you* are very conscious of time, and that you plan to keep the ideas marching briskly along.

Watch your time. Nothing strikes as responsive a chord with the businessman as time! He has been made very conscious of the time element by the fact that the day is too short for him to get all his work done. Any attempt to give him more time for his work will receive his warm appreciation. Time is a sensitive area. Ask him!

Business meetings waste time indiscriminately. Make your meetings different. If you can reverse this trend, you will get broad support from the group. They will come better prepared. They will hold closer to the subject, mainly because they won't be worn out by endless, aimless talk. As a result, they will move more directly to solutions and avoid wasteful tangents.

Set the *time* standard. Everyone stands to gain!

Suggestion: Keep the promise you made when you sent out the agenda. Keep to your stated time limit. If the meeting drags, move in quickly. Make it absolutely clear that you plan to work within the time you established. Nothing can make you more popular.

The role of the leader calls for great versatility,

flexibility, and perception. Add to these an understanding of people and the realization that they can't all possibly see everything the same way.

One last suggestion. When you are called to lead a meeting, lead it. There are times when the leader fails to exert control and one of the meeting members takes over. This doesn't rectify the situation . . . it just means the wrong man was chosen to be leader.

|||| LEADERSHIP AT THE CLOSE
OF THE MEETING

"Let us hear the conclusion of the whole matter."

—*Old Testament*

The closing of the meeting is the pay-off. Everything done up to this minute has been directed to this end. And here too often, "for the want of a nail, the shoe was lost."

The closing of the meeting places special demands on the leader. Good guidance has brought the group to a solution of the problem. Now is the time to nail down the decision. Without a firm hand by the leader, the results can easily be lost or buried by misdirection.

At the close of the meeting the discussion is over. The leader now takes a position of complete authority. He reports directly the conclusions reached, the major disagreements, and most important, the future steps to be taken.

The following suggestions will help you fulfill completely your job as leader at the end of the meeting.

Point out the decisions reached. A clear statement of the decisions of the meeting recalls for the last time the agreements made. It gets the conclusions out in the open before the group. In the heat of discussion it's easy to lose track of agreed-upon ideas. A summary will spotlight them.

The summary of decisions reached in the meeting will bring to surface any individual misunderstandings and disagreements. Naturally, this helps avoid additional unnecessary meetings.

Point out differences. Obviously, all meetings cannot be expected to end in complete agreement. The disagreements will be vital to future discussions. State them clearly. Evaluate the disagreements; indicate if they are small or great.

Try to define them to the satisfaction of all present, particularly the minority group. Remember, you will have to deal with the minority in the next meeting, and that meeting will go more smoothly if they feel they have been given a fair shake!

Point to future action. State clearly the next steps to be taken. Announce if another meeting will be necessary. And when! Indicate how the decisions reached at *this* meeting will be used in the overall project. Thank the members for their help.

Follow up the meeting with a written confirmation of the decisions reached and the future action to be taken. This will serve as a reminder of the results to the meeting members, and will inform other personnel who are interested but not personally involved in this particular meeting.

Always stress the positive!

The leader has concluded a successful meeting.

"The horror of that moment," the
King went on, "I shall never, never *for-*
get!"
"You will though," the Queen said, *"if
you don't make a memorandum of it."*
—Alice's Adventures in Wonderland

The Queen was absolutely right. He will forget
unless he gets it down on paper.

This quote was taken from perhaps the most
famous book on communication in the English
language, Lewis Carroll's *Alice's Adventures in
Wonderland*. The situation he refers to above is a
telling comment on something that happens every
day in business. Ideas are not put on paper and are
lost or forgotten. As a result, they must be found
again! This calls for an additional and unnecessary
investment of valuable time.

It's easy for the results of a meeting to slip
away. Therefore, always end your meeting plan
with the following rule: "Get the results down on

paper."

Suggestion: Set up a standard form for the meeting-following memo. Make it short. Make it simple. But, make it standard! Insist that everyone in the organization follow it.

Try one like this:

Date of Meeting _____

Name of sender _____

Where held _____

People present _____

Subject _____

Conclusions reached _____

Future action _____

This memo will nail down the positive steps taken at the meeting. It will hold the line at the point where the meeting ended and will avoid slipping back. It will point to what must be done next. It will prevent you, like the King, from forgetting!

IIII USING THE "SOLUTION WHEEL"
FOR PROBLEM SOLVING

Too many meetings eat up valuable time tacking back and forth in the breeze of undirected talk. These soothing drafts of casual chatter clutter up the thinking of the group and gently lull them into a state of inaction.

If the meeting is to be used in business, it must have a form. It must clearly point the way to quick and accurate decisions. Remember, in business, the goal of the meeting is seldom knowledge . . . it is usually action.

The "solution wheel" guide is designed to direct the solving of problems in the business meeting. It is a road map from problem to solution, from need to action, from question to decision.

The "solution wheel" has a place in every company; in every meeting room. Read the description of this aid in the next several pages; then have some made up for your organization. Make them big and pin one up in each meeting room. Use it as a guide in all meetings for a week. The results will surprise you—pleasantly!

Here's what the "solution wheel" guide will do:

It will give the leader a clear-cut plan for the meeting. It will give him a specific outline for a flexible speech situation.

It will show the individual member of the meeting exactly where the subject stands and what still has to be done to solve the problem.

It will get *all* the information out and *all* the questions answered *in the right order*. This is one of the major meeting stumbling blocks. The foundation of facts are seldom aired sufficiently to provide a solid base for solution.

The "solution wheel" will establish a pattern for company meetings which will take hold and eventually be universally used. When everyone understands the direction the meeting should take, "meeting teams" will unconsciously form.

Meetings will begin to jell and move directly to solutions.

All the people closely concerned with the meeting situation will lose the feeling that the meetings are not moving logically. With it will go the hopeless belief that the meeting can never accomplish anything. They will know that a carefully thought out form is being followed, a form which has a definite purpose and direction. They will know that it is a form that works and will make their day more pleasant and profitable.

The "solution wheel" is a guide to direct talk. Here's how it works:

Step 1. "What is the problem?"

At the opening of the meeting, this is the question the "solution wheel" asks.

The leader fulfills step 1 in the "solution wheel" pattern by:

1. Clearly stating the problem.

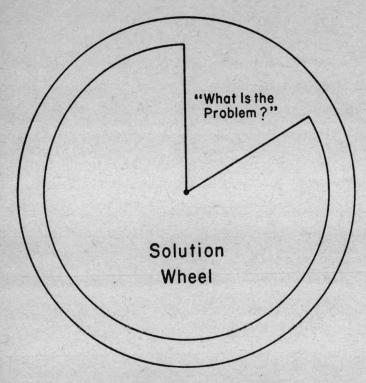

2. Limiting the subject if possible.
3. Defining the problem by using examples, illustrations, etc.
4. Showing the scope of the problem.

Step 2.   "How did we get here?"
Next, background information must come out.
As leader, ask the following questions:

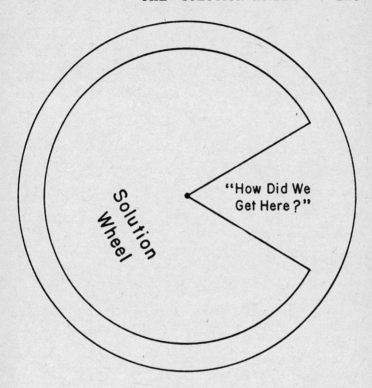

1. "What do we know *about* the problem?"
2. "How *long* has it existed?"
3. "What brought the problem into being?"
4. "What are the effects of the problem we see now?"

5. "What do we *think* will be the effects of the problem?"

Step 3.   "Where do we want to come out?"
At this point the goal must be clearly stated!
Level in on what you hope to achieve in the meeting. You have small chance of success unless

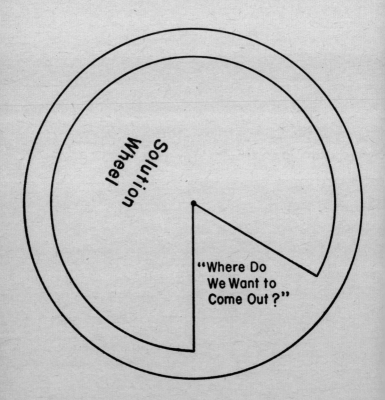

the acceptable solutions are talked about. Ask,

    1. "What's the complete solution?"

    2. "What guideposts will tell us we are close to an acceptable solution?"

    3. "What compromise solution will do?"

Step 4. *"There are several possible answers."* Every problem can be resolved in several differ-

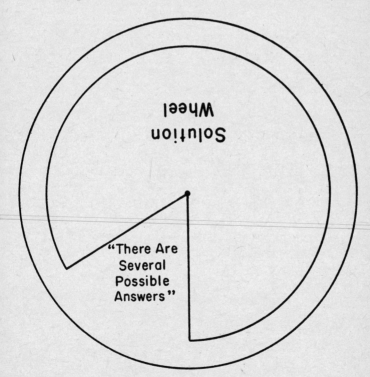

ent ways. The key is to look at them all and choose the best!

Now comes the flood! Almost everyone has solutions. Draw out the group by questioning:

1. "What must an acceptable solution do?"
2. "How many solutions are feasible?"
3. "What are the drawbacks?"
4. "Is there a *combined* solution?"
5. "Let's look back again at the criteria we set up earlier!"

Step 5. *"Which is the best?"*

You can look at all the solutions, but finally you must choose one. The one best suited to do the job!

All the efforts of your meeting group have been directed to this goal—the solving of the question at hand. Again, the leader must nail it down. Ask these questions . . . in this order:

1. "What solution do you think is best?"
2. "Can we *all* agree on this plan?"

NOW STATE THE SOLUTION IN A CLEAR VOICE!!!!!

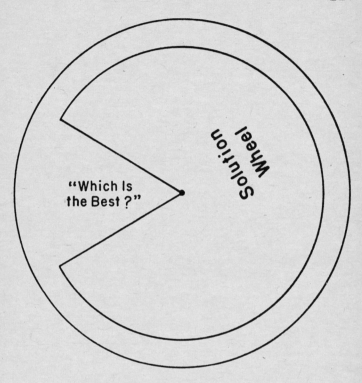

Step 6.   *"Now we have it, let's try it!"*

This step points the way to the application of the meeting solution and future action.

Too many people leave the meeting room without knowing how to use what they've resolved. Too

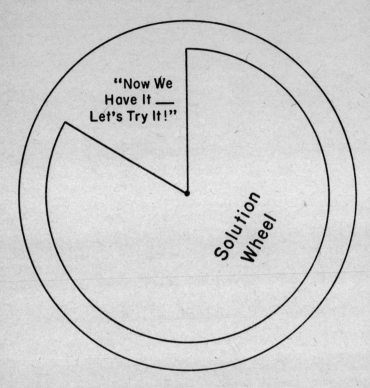

many meetings end without deciding *how, where,* and *when,* to apply the solution! Say,

"We have the answer. We know what we want to do. Who's going to put it to work? And when?"

The meeting has been brought to a successful end!

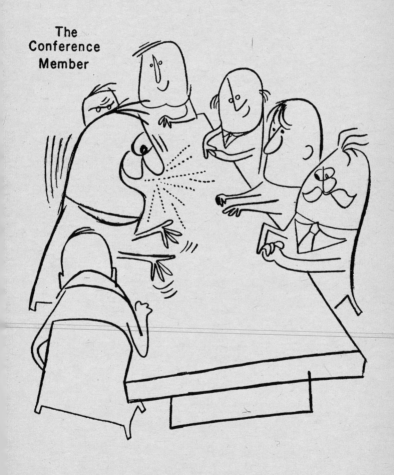

119

|||| HOW TO PREPARE FOR THE MEETING

Herbert Hoover said, "Facts don't threaten, they operate."

He was talking about the surest way to success in any meeting—ammunition. The ammunition you gather from careful preparation! This is the one ingredient for which there is no substitute. The man with the facts can make his point of view prevail at any time. Have the facts to hammer home your stand in the next meeting!

Most meetings last too long. At least 60 percent of all meeting members sit down at the table poorly prepared. There is a definite connection between the two.

If there is any magic path to shorter meetings,

it is to do everything possible to see that the meeting members have reviewed the subject *thoroughly* before the meeting.

Here are suggestions to guide your preparation for your next meeting. They will make your contributions more valuable. They will make your meetings more profitable and pleasant. They will make them shorter!

1. Look over the subject and be sure you know your own point of view. Determine definitely where you want to come out. You may choose to change your direction in the course of the meeting, but you *must* have an initial goal.

2. Estimate what opposition you might meet. Everyone can judge what the opposing points of view will be. Evaluate their validity and strength. Determine beforehand how you will confront them.

3. Examine the "solution wheel" steps from problem to solution. If you

know the answer to the problem being discussed, be sure you can prove it!

4. Pick up information and strengthen your contributions for each step. Many a good idea has died for want of nourishment. Be sure *you* support yours.

5. Examine possible compromises. Come to the meeting with alternative solutions—solutions you know will satisfy all conflicting parties. Don't expect the impossible. There are many times when the whole problem cannot be solved in one meeting. Compromise—resolve it in the next meeting!

Next time a meeting is called, review the above suggestions. Apply them. You'll see that they work!

IIII HOW TO CONTRIBUTE
IN THE MEETING

There are three types of statements you can make in your meetings. Each can help you resolve the problem at hand. Each can successfully move the meeting forward. However, you must learn to recognize each type and get to know how to use it productively.

Here are the three statement types:

1. *Statements of Fact.* These are the building blocks of any form of communication. They form a solid base for your meeting. They are contributions of facts, statistics, illustrations, comparisons, etc., which can be put together to illuminate and define the subject being discussed. They are statements your listeners will feel they can accept because they can be checked. Not that the meeting members will jump up and rush out to verify your information—but they will recognize the factual matter as

being available for their review. Discussions revolving on statements of fact usually meet with little trouble. Most people can come to agree on facts!

Suggestion: Stay with statements of fact until the problem has been fully aired. This approach will get your meeting off to a solid start. In addition, it will discourage "flash solutions" which commonly come right at the opening of the meeting and so often serve only to lead the group off on tangents.

2. *Statements of Evaluation*. These are statements that can only be made based on the statements of fact. It follows that they should not be made until *all* the facts are out. Statements of evaluation are interpretations and opinions of facts and are frequently strongly supported by emotions. Watch them! It is in this area that the leader

must be very alert for conflicts. It is
almost impossible to pin down or
prove a statement of evaluation. Except—and this is the secret—by going
back to reëxamine the facts!

3. *Statements of Policy.* This is the pay-
off! This is the problem-solving
offering. These statements point out
directions to be taken, ways the problem can be handled. Obviously, statements of policy can only come at the
end of the meeting. They *must* be built
on facts and evaluations of facts.

The development of *any* idea or the solving of
any problem has three definite stages. The examination of the facts; the evaluation of the facts;
and, finally, *action.*

Here again are the contributions that lead to
decisions:

1. *Statements of Facts*
2. *Statements of Evaluation*
3. *Statements of Policy*

IIII HOW TO ORGANIZE YOUR CONTRIBUTION

The meeting table speaking situation is designed to stimulate the joint building of ideas by a group of people. It sets one thought on another, qualifies the preceding concept, points to the following decision. It is a very complex operation.

Each member of the meeting may make 25 or 30 contributions in an hour. Each contribution is evaluated, considered, meshed into the overall subject. Every contribution, whether used or not, has its effect on the direction and length of the meeting.

And none of this information has any more permanent form than the thoughts in the minds of the individual meeting members. Obviously, the ideas must be presented directly and clearly.

Simplicity of statement and organization *must* be the keynote!

Use a contribution form like this:

    1. STATEMENT OF FACT—EVALUATION

—POLICY

Followed by:

2. SUPPORT OF STATEMENT

Followed by:

3. RESTATEMENT OF FACT—EVALUA-
   TION—POLICY

It's the old rule for public speakers:

"Tell 'em what you're going to tell 'em!"

"Tell 'em!"

"Tell 'em what you told 'em!"

Keep your statement to *one* key idea. Two ideas are often just enough to derail the thinking of the group. You'll have many more chances to speak up!

Another suggestion: Keep your contribution short. 25 to 40 words. One-half minute at the most.

Too simple? That's impossible! It can't be *too* simple.

Here again is the direct form for presenting an idea in a meeting:

1. STATEMENT OF FACT—EVALUATION
   —POLICY

2. SUPPORT OF STATEMENT

3. RESTATEMENT OF FACT—EVALUATION—POLICY

Let's look at the second step, the support step.

This step has only one purpose: to win an acceptance from the group for your point of view or idea. It is designed to make the meeting believe you and to use your contribution as a forward step on the path from problem to solution.

You have stated your point; now support it with . . .

—STATISTICS

(Make them simple and brief!)

—DRAMATIZED FIGURES

"If we used that money in advertising, we could put our sales message into 95 percent of the homes in America."

—EXAMPLES

"For instance, if the plant's production line was extended, we could produce X number more boxes between now and Christmas."

—COMPARISONS

"Only last year three competitive brands came on the market in larger cases. They had no trouble getting dealers to accept them."

—SIMILES AND ANALOGIES

"We're like the British before the battle of Taranto; we're so out-numbered we can do nothing but attack."

—VISUALS

(Nothing persuades like that which you can see. Too few visuals are used at meetings. Try them, they'll win your point.)

—HUMOROUS STORY

(This is a vital tool in *any* speech situation. Everyone needs to relax! Use humor to reduce the tension and to give all concerned a breather.)

Use these supports, and they will help you sell your ideas simply and directly.

Use these ideas, and people will listen to your points . . . and remember them!

IIII ARE YOU SURE YOU DISAGREE?

"No one means all he says, and very few say all they mean, for words are slippery and thought is viscous."
—*Henry Brooks Adams*

Mr. Adams, all philosophers, historians, teachers, and students of language, find it necessary at some time or other to point out this basic truth: language is an inadequate means of passing an idea. One more time won't hurt!

A great many conflicts around the meeting table result from an idea that has changed in meaning in the trip from speaker to listener. Two people arguing about two interpretations of the same idea take a long time to come together!

Let's look at some things that cause misunderstanding in talk between people and see how they can be avoided.

Here's what happens when someone decides to

pass an idea. The thought comes into his mind. To give it to someone else, he must put it into a form which can be passed to his listener . . . speech. To frame the idea to be spoken, he must transpose the thought into symbols (words), and then speak them. The listener must then translate the symbols (words) and try to come out with the full meaning of the original idea.

You can see that the system is full of traps!

For instance: the idea may not be completely clear in the mind of the speaker. Or, in framing the idea, the speaker may choose the wrong words. Or, it is possible that the listener may make the wrong translation.

And remember, the slightest variation in meaning can cause the most violent conflict!

Here are some things that set up time-consuming and emotion-exhausting misunderstandings:

Misunderstanding of a word. Words are the idea carriers. They are also major culprits in causing disagreements. When you prepare to pass an idea, take just a moment more of time to be sure you are

Are You Sure You Disagree?

as close to the true meaning as possible. Be sure you are using the simplest, clearest words you can find to do the job. Avoid "hedge" words, indefinite words, jargon. Use crisp words and keep your sentences short!

Misunderstanding of the tone of voice. The words are not the only workers in projecting a thought. The words are spoken in a vocal tone that sets up much of the meaning. How many times have you heard people say,

"I don't like the way he said that."

They are talking about the tone of the speaker's voice.

Be sure your speaking tone is not misleading. You can help avoid misunderstanding by sticking with straight simple word sentences and working for a voice that by variety presents the idea and the emotional feeling behind the idea, thus helping to translate the thought for the listener. At the same time, avoid fine-line subtlety, satire, and irony. Make the ultimate goal clarity.

Misunderstanding of degree of feeling. Many meeting members speak with a studied monotone of voice. This seems to be taken by many businessmen as a sign of mental strength. Unfortunately, this lack of variety in the voice means the signposts that point out the meaning of the thought have been taken down! A voice with no inflection, no emotion, frequently makes the listener ask, "Now what does he mean? How does he stand on that? How strongly does he hold to that position?"

Suggestion: Don't camouflage your voice. Use every device at your control to make your meaning more clear. Make your voice say what you really mean.

One final suggestion. The listener has a very important job. He must work just as hard as the speaker to be sure he has received the correct thought. Listening is never a passive activity.

‖‖ THE GOOD VOICE IN CONFERENCE

"Speak the speech, I pray you, trippingly on the tongue."

Hamlet's request to the visiting players has become the plea of countless people whose lives are made up of talking together. If the ideas are the raw material, the voice is the machine that molds them, shapes them, offers them in a working form. Be sure your voice machine is adjusted to equal the quality of the basic idea.

Many a good idea has died for the want of a good presentation!

Check yourself on the following good vocal qualities:

DICTION   Speak clearly. Form each word fully. Don't slur syllables. Watch words that end in a sounded p, b, t, d, k, g; be sure you make them crisply. If you really want a superior voice, take some speech lessons. Good speech is one of your most valuable attributes.

PROJECTION Speak out! They can't believe you if they can't hear you. Look at your fellow members in the meeting. Speak your ideas to each of them. Give each a line. People respect speakers who look them in the eye; they believe speakers who use the personal attention approach.

RATE Most speakers talk too fast. They seem to want to get it over with! Don't destroy a thought or throw

away an idea by not giv-
ing it the time it deserves.
Test your own rate. Speak
a passage for one minute.
If you cover more than
160 words, you're going
too fast. If you're under
120, too slow. Practice and
apply the right rate to
your next meeting and
note how your ideas stick.

VARIETY   Variety is change. Change
is the basic material of
interest and excitement.
Don't allow your voice to
work on one monotonous
pitch level. The droning
voice is deadly effective
in its ability to smother a
good idea. Don't let this
happen to you. Practice
variety by reading aloud.
Make your wife and kids

listen. Work for upward and downward inflections that make the words you say carry more meaning. That is the goal . . . more meaning.

Perhaps you can pick up a tape recorder and record your voice. If you do, you will recognize immediately how much more expressive your speaking voice can be. If you don't know how to improve, see a speech specialist. You can get advice at your nearest university.

If you apply the above suggestions you will be a more interesting and effective meeting speaker. If others do it too, *you* will enjoy your meetings more!

‖‖ WORDS . . . WORDS . . . WORDS

When Alice met Humpty-Dumpty, he proceeded to make his ideas about language very plain.

"When I use a word, it means just what *I* choose it to mean, neither more nor less."

A wonderful thought. It would make the world quite different, but unfortunately words do not mean just what we choose them to mean. We must choose just the right words, and use them in just the right combination, if we want to communicate clearly and without confusion.

The following ideas may help you use words that mean the same to *everyone* in the meeting. And *that* is the goal!

Be sure you use the simplest, most direct words you know. Don't strive for polish; work for clarity.

Use short sentences. Depend primarily on declarative sentences. And keep them down to 15 words if possible. Avoid starting with a subordinate clause, i.e., "if this is to work, etc." This more complex form just places one more barrier in the way of understanding, and the meeting has plenty without an additional one.

Be concrete. Avoid the abstract. The unspecific always means that your listeners must make one more translation to wring out the meaning.

Avoid irony. Most groups won't get it!

Minimize the use of rhetorical questions. It's true that this device can be effectively used to pull out more information on a subject; however, a statement can usually be used with more profit. Many members hide behind the rhetorical question and snipe rather than contribute. For example, "Do you mean you think that will work?"

Use vivid words. A striking phrase or word sticks in the minds of the meeting members. They will remember it and therefore the idea you proposed. If they remember, they may accept. If they accept, they may act the way you suggest. After your next meeting, try to remember the most vivid contribution made. It was probably the idea that prevailed!

If an idea is not clear, question. What is unclear to you is very likely being lost to the entire group.

Dullness is one of the plagues of the meeting. Vivid wording of clear thinking can quickly do away with this disease.

‖‖ ONE FINAL NOTE—
DIPLOMACY

Much has been asked and more has been written about interpersonal relations between members of the meeting group. About everyone getting along well. About handling the difficult member.

This author believes that these problems are bound to exist whenever thinking people holding strong ideas talk together. To try to analyze each problem by type and individual can be like chasing a will-of-the-wisp.

If, however, the meeting has direction, good leadership, and a clearly defined goal, these problems tend to solve themselves.

Here, are some last suggestions:

Listen with respect to all contributions.

Discuss; don't argue about points.

Ask difficult members to explain, and explain, and explain, etc.

Try to get out of the emotional sphere and into the factual.

Allow members to save face. You may be talking to them again tomorrow.

Your meetings *must* become a more effective tool for you and your company. They are a tool that *can* be extremely efficient and productive.

There is very little choice, since the conference has no substitute.

"*In that case,*" *said the Dodo solemnly, rising to its feet,* "*I move the meeting adjourn, for the immediate adoption of more energetic remedies—*"

"*Speak English!*" *said the Eaglet.* "*I don't know the meaning of half those long words, and, what's more, I don't believe you do, either.*"

—*Alice's Adventures in Wonderland*